american
sacred choral music

AN OVERVIEW AND HANDBOOK

Samuel Adler • Craig Timberlake
James E. Jordan, Jr. • David Chalmers
Introduction by Daniel Pinkham

PARACLETE PRESS
Brewster, Massachusetts

Library of Congress Cataloging-in-Publication Data

American sacred choral music : overview and handbook / Samuel Adler
. . . [et al.].
     p. cm.
Includes bibliographical references (p. 74).
ISBN 1-55725-276-9 (trade paper)
1. Church music—United States. 2. Choral singing—Instruction
and study. 3. Synagogue music—United States—History and criticism.
I. Adler, Samuel, 1928-   .
  ML2911 .A45 2001
  782.5'22'0973—dc21

2001002609

10 9 8 7 6 5 4 3 2 1

© 2001 by Gloriæ Dei Cantores
ISBN: 1-55725-276-9

Published by Paraclete Press
Brewster, Massachusetts
www.paracletepress.com
Printed in the United States of America.

Table of Contents

Foreword

My own journey into the world of American sacred music began at the urging of a dear friend and colleague, Dr. Craig Timberlake. For a considerable time I had been luxuriating in the sounds of the English and European choral traditions, discovering the literature available and some that had been lost behind what was then the "Iron Curtain." The numerous tours of *Gloriæ Dei Cantores* throughout Europe (both western and eastern), Russia, and the British Isles required an ever-deepening exploration into the unique character and diversity of sacred music in those regions, a task to which I was more than happy to give myself. Those were exhilarating times indeed.

The vigorous demands this task placed upon our singers prompted me to request of Craig some comprehensive direction in the area of vocal care (only one of his many specialties). He gave more than I asked or expected, gladly offering his pedagogical counsel while also nudging me to enlarge our musical exploration with the rich heritage of sacred music in America—what he calls "the unending chorus of praise to God of the so-called New World." Packets of choral literature, carefully collected and ordered, began to arrive. Thus, a new adventure began, and I and *Gloriæ Dei Cantores* will be forever indebted to this fine scholar and gentleman.

The living faith of our forebears, and its influence on the formation of this nation and culture, have marked a unique place in human history. The religious freedoms expressed by her laws and enjoyed by her people have helped to found America on the noble idea that divine principles and human dignity are inherently related. And her sacred songs have aptly given voice to this idea from one generation to the next. My own faith was strengthened and informed as I made this journey, retrieving the roots and retracing the steps of sacred music's evolution in America. The more I discovered, the more committed I became to shouldering our own corner of responsibility for preserving and advancing this heritage. Moreover, returning to our earliest music has led us steadfastly to the present, and to the contributions of so many other nationalities who, in joining this nation of religious freedoms, became Americans themselves and contributed new musical ideas and sounds. We are blessed with a rare and wonderful national treasure.

This little book springs from a desire to share this treasure. Perhaps by reading it, others also will feel moved to rediscover the beliefs and personalities of a nation's people of faith, together with the ideas, the movements, and the thoughts that shaped both the performers and the composers of America's religious music.

Elizabeth Patterson
Director, Gloriæ Dei Cantores
February, 2001

Introduction

Daniel Pinkham

It is encouraging for me to see the continuing and vibrant interest in sacred choral music in America. A paradox strikes us, however, when we recognize that this great repertoire may be rejected in the very sanctuaries for which it was intended. There will always be some critics who declare that we should not have "performances" in churches and synagogues that call attention to the glories of the art of music. Tolstoy wrote that "Art is a human activity having for its purpose the transmission to others of the highest and best feelings to which man has risen." I must confess that after serving churches for over sixty years, I still feel the greatest sense of spiritual involvement from the art of sacred music.

I would like to cite a couple of examples in response to the demand for the familiar. Much music (and this is particularly true of either very old or very new works) sounds like a foreign language, and its vocabulary and syntax sound forbidding. We can hear a recently discovered Mozart or Haydn work and listen with pleasure, because we already know the composer's language. Through many rehearsals, the performers learn the language and are reconciled to its challenges. The audience, alas, may get to hear this music but once. They have no means of translating this new language into their comprehension.

I recall hearing the premiere of Bartok's *Concerto for Orchestra*. The conductor, Serge Koussevitsky, had commissioned the work for the Boston Symphony Orchestra and was convinced of its worth. The critics savaged the work, and the audience reaction was hostile. Nevertheless, Koussevitsky was committed to the work and, as a matter of both defiance and conviction, he programmed the same work for the very next concert. This time, the audience and the critics were moved to enthusiasm. The work is, of course, now one of the most popular pieces from the middle of the twentieth century.

At King's Chapel in the early 1960s, I programmed Richard Felciano's *Pentecost Sunday,* a colorful and bold work for chorus, organ, and electronic tape. During the week before, the order of service announced this new and experimental work and invited interested members of the congregation to hear the rehearsal before the service. It was also announced that following the postlude the work would be performed again. A very old lady came up to me afterwards to say that she had never before so clearly appreciated the drama of the text from *Acts.* She had heard the work at both the rehearsal and the performances.

A colleague told me of his going as a substitute teacher to run a chorus in an inner-city school. Attendance at chorus was a requirement. The previous teacher, who had performed music based on pop taste, had recently resigned. My colleague had a very radical point of view: since the students hated these rehearsals but had to be there anyway, he decided to do repertoire that would give him pleasure and to which he was committed. He elected to work on a Bach cantata. Not only did attendance improve, but also the students became involved in the music, unconsciously recognizing the happy balance of heart and head. The "foreign language" had been learned, and with it came the pleasures of the literature.

In the era of Mozart and Haydn it was a normal procedure to compose a work on commission from a wealthy patron. Today, commissions come from foundations, educational institutions, or performing groups, and occasionally from the performers themselves. Churches and synagogues have also been known to offer commissions. One of my most memorable experiences came from a commission from the Temple at University Circle in Cleveland. They had a well-endowed fund that annually commissioned a Sacred Service from, in alternate years, either a Jewish composer or a non-Jewish composer. This commission afforded me the chance to learn about a new liturgy and to work in a new language, namely Hebrew. It brought to the synagogue a familiar text but in an unusual yet sincere musical language.

In 1962, the Ford Foundation gave me a generous grant by which I was able to commission four Americans: Ned Rorem, Ulysses Kay, William Flanagan, and Charles Wuorinen. The commission specified a work for SATB of college or community chorus level. The accompaniment was to be for string quintet of advanced professional caliber. Each of the four composers came to Boston for an hour-long broadcast over WGBH public radio. The programs began with an interview with the composer, followed by a "rehearsal" in which various sections of the work were performed and then discussed. Then the work was performed in its entirety. We subsequently performed the works as a concert in both New York and in King's Chapel and ultimately all four works were released by Cambridge Records, a disc long out of print. I was delighted that Ned Rorem's work *Two Psalms and a Proverb* was published by E.C. Schirmer Music.

Fortunately, it does not require a Ford Foundation to set wheels in motion. If you have a viable musical program in your church or synagogue, have your local composer write something for the singers. Invite your composer to hear a rehearsal so that he can find the strengths (or weaknesses) of your chorus. Too few men? SAB repertoire is always acceptable. Are there instrumentalists in your congregation? Even a simple obbligato or interlude can make the new work more colorful. This experience will at once be of interest to the singers as participants in the creative act, and will also afford the composer a realistic lesson on writing for amateur singers. Walter Piston once told me that he had learned much from having written, as a young composer, a work for the Pierian Sodality of 1808, the Harvard University student orchestra. It taught him how to make an amateur orchestra sound good by idiomatic writing for the various instruments. Were this well-written piece to be played by the Boston Symphony, it would, of course, sound even better.

I am a great believer in program notes. Even when a performance of the composition is weak, I find great solace in them. With a new work, be sure that the audience has texts and translations. Let them know something about the composer: his education, influences, and style. If it is possible, get some quotes from the composer. Also, get quotes from the singers, because they, after all, will be intimately involved.

After sixty years of serving as organist and music director in various churches, I have now retired from that "contact sport." However, my interest in the potential for excellence in musical programs has not diminished. I still relish hearing new works. I still feel enlightened by the vision of young composers. I still strongly encourage churches and synagogues to proceed with a commissioning project. One word of advice, however, is not out of place: Do not ever tell anybody that it is their moral duty to program new works; rather, tell them that you do it because it gives you and others great pleasure.

Harmonia Americana
our legacy of sacred music

Craig Timberlake

In 1992, the Quincentenary celebration of Columbus's voyage of discovery to the New World provided dissidents, revisionists, and interest groups of every persuasion with yet another opportunity to lament the despoliation of the Western Hemisphere and the destruction of ancient cultures by dubious representatives of European civilization in general and the Western church in particular.

Of course there are countless grains of truth in the many indictments over the centuries that have cited rape, pillage, bigotry, intolerance, disease, death, and destruction. In the Columbian anniversary observances, many people undoubtedly followed with lively interest the swelling chorus of complaints against man's inhumanity to man in pursuit of his perceived duty to God. *Plus ça change, plus c'est la même chose.* Indeed it does often appear that evil and its manifestations are immutable. But there is another chorus that absorbs this writer's attention in the brief observations that follow—the unending chorus of praise to God of the so-called New World in the five centuries from the time of Columbus to contemporary Columbia (the U.S.A.) and its neighbors.

1

Following the conquest of Mexico by Cortes and subjugation of the Aztec Empire (1521), the reverend Fathers, bearing the cross and obedient to their divine mission to convert the heathen, taught Indian boys to join them in singing the liturgical music of the church. An *Ordinarium* appeared in 1556. It was the first book with music to be printed in the New World. Among the compositions of Hernando Franco, one-time chapel master of the Mexico City Cathedral (c. 1575–1585), are two hymns to the Virgin in the Indian language *Nahuatl*. Today, thanks to the untiring efforts of musicologists, we can perform the Latin masses, magnificats, psalms, and responsories that comprise the Mexican polyphonic music composed in the New World.

In the northeastern United States, our Pilgrim and Puritan forebears brought with them their English psalters, *Ainsworth* (1612) and *Sternhold and Hopkins* (1562), in which the metric paraphrases of psalms were often sung to lively and spirited tunes, some of secular origin. To the modern ear those tunes seem only to point up the awkward construction and ineptitude of these paraphrases or translations for singing. No wonder John Cotton and twenty-nine other New England divines tried their hand at the improved versions of the psalms that comprised the *Bay Psalm Book* of 1640, a work immediately adopted by congregations of the Massachusetts Bay Colony. Plymouth followed suit in 1692, the year, incidentally, of the Salem witchcraft trials, when twenty condemned witches were hanged, before the church leaders and the populace came to their senses.

By the end of the seventeenth century, the deterioration of psalm singing (brought about in part by a decline in music literacy) and the thrust for reform delivered by young ministerial graduates of Harvard led ultimately to an eighteenth century of remarkable creativity and enterprise. Singing schools and amateur composers sprang up in New England and in the rest of the Northeast. They came from all walks of life: clergymen, tanners, farmers, schoolteachers, and politicians. Tunebooks flourished. These "open-enders" or "long boys" offered a new American repertoire of hymns, "fuging" tunes, and anthems.

Among our first American composers were James Read, Andrew Law, Daniel Read, Timothy Swan, Samuel Holyoke, Oliver Holden, Supply Belcher, and William Billings. Much of their long-neglected music we find today to be vibrant, energetic, and vivacious, going its melodious way indifferent to European common practice with its rules of voice-leading and harmonic progression. Such free spirits were bound to incur the disapproval and displeasure of nineteenth-century educators and tastemakers, and their works fell into neglect as the regulators encouraged and put forth bland imitations of the European style, and, even worse, arrangements of works by such masters as Handel, Haydn, Beethoven, and Mozart.

The tension between the vernacular and the cultivated styles, and the popular and the learned tradition, has been a recurrent theme in American sacred music. While America's classically trained composers and performers went to Europe to be finished off, our Yankee tunesmiths went South in the pages of shape-note song collections and others: *Kentucky Harmony, Southern Harmony, The Sacred Harp*. In the last named we find five examples of Billings in shape notes of the fasola tradition.

Among the earlier Christian sects, the Moravians brought the most highly developed musical culture to America. Choirs differentiated by age, sex, and marital status conducted their own devotionals and festivals. Orchestras and choirs joined in the *Liebesmahl,* or Love Feast, and Christian music education was richly and systematically developed. American-born Moravian composers enriched our repertoire of sacred music for over a hundred years before economic conditions, changing tastes, and increasing secularization reduced their creative abundance.

While the celibate Shaker colonies lasted for over two hundred years, their numbers dwindled rapidly for lack of converts. Their considerable vernacular hymnody enriches American sacred song. As the religious historian Martin Marty wrote: "Despite their failure, however, many Americans today still admire the directness and clarity of their expressions in song, tools, and furniture." Above all they had the "gift to be simple. . .to come down where we ought to be."

America's most significant contributions to hymnody are generally considered to be the gospel hymns emerging from the nineteenth-century revivalist movement, along with the spirituals, black and white, of the deep South, whose connections to secular folksong have been argued in an extensive literature.

It is in hymns of the church that we encounter a thriving musical ecumenism. Take *The Hymnal 1982* of the Episcopal Church. Here we have Billings beside the Hebrew round "Shalom chaverim." *The Kentucky Harmony, Sacred Harmony,* and *The Sacred Harp* are all represented, as are Anglican chant, plainsong, and the Lutheran chorale.

For the church musician, the ecumenical content of the great hymnals of our various denominations provides not only inspiration but also a remarkable reference, as we endeavor to balance the participation and performance of choir, liturgists (where appropriate), and congregation in musical worship. The extent of the problem is suggested in this favorite passage from Robert Stevenson's *Protestant Church Music in America* (1966):

> So long as America continues diverse enough to be a land in which more than 250 denominations can flourish, church music will probably continue to reflect all the amazing varieties of social background, wealth, education, and aspiration that have called this plethora of religious bodies into being and made their continued

support possible. In one sense, this diversity is much to be desired. In a day when uniformity swamps so many other aspects of American life, at least church music can continue to boast of ranging everywhere from the cheaply vulgar to the expensively sublime. (p.128).

Stevenson's work is a useful *Short Survey of Men and Movements from 1564 to the Present,* as its subtitle reads. Church musicians rarely have the time to indulge a taste for historical research, but his selective bibliography can be of genuine service. One may, for example, find oneself responsive to the evidence of burgeoning research after World War II, but unable to devote time to find and read the tastemakers— Lowell Mason, George Hood in his *A History of Music in New England* (1846), and Thomas Hasting in his *Dissertation on Musical Taste* (1822, 1857). These did not share our enthusiasm for the Yankee tunesmiths, such as William Billings, Supply Belcher, et al.—American originals, whose musical "ineptitude" is overcome by their enterprise, originality, and melodic and rhythmic invention.

It should be noted that Stevenson's bibliography includes Canon Charles Winfred Douglas's *Church Music in History and Practice* (1937, 1962). If you can find it, this is the classic treatment of the origins and expansions of the liturgical church. Though addressed to Episcopalians, it is of great benefit to all interested church musicians. Leonard Ellinwood, who edited the revised edition, added a tenth chapter entitled, "The Praise of God Today."

There are other pertinent histories, such as Gilbert Chase's classic, *American Music,* which make clear that the Puritans were not opposed to instrumental music outside the church, and part singing was not totally unknown. In addition to their psalters, the Puritans and Pilgrims could have known Thomas Ravencroft's *Whole Booke of Psalms* (London,

1621), containing four-part settings of the British psalm-tune repertory for recreational use. Superior voices and instrumental skills were surely appreciated then as in any age.

Samuel Sewall (1652–1730) resigned his precentor's place in Old South Church in favor of a better singer, the tallow chandler Josiah Franklin, young Benjamin Franklin's father. Many years later, Franklin wrote that his father's voice "was sonorous and agreeable; so that when he sung a psalm or hymn, with the accompaniment of his violin, with which he sometimes amused himself in an evening after the labors of the day were finished, it was truly delightful to hear him." (Stevenson, p.18) Thomas Jefferson is known to have had a clear tenor voice, to have practiced the violin three hours a day, and to have written the words under the notes in a collection of psalm tunes found in his music library.

Leaving the historical realm, one has to cite such indispensable sources as Irving Lowens's *Music and Musicians in Early America* and, in *The New Grove Dictionary of American Music,* such articles as "Psalmody," "Hymnody," and "Psalms, metrical." A relatively complete picture then emerges of sacred music in Colonial America.

Twentieth-century American church music is altogether remarkable, in my judgment. If you have an opportunity to hear *Gloriæ Dei Cantores'* recordings of American psalmody, you will, I am sure, agree that music of such beauty, craftsmanship, and choral/instrumental art should be preserved into the third millenium. The goal of the church musician then must be to pursue traditional means and to elevate those standards of excellence that set apart our music for worship from the music of everyday life.

In his chronology, *A Chronicle of American Music 1700–1995,* Charles Hall dutifully records accomplishments in two domains: "The Vernacular/Commercial Scene" vs. "The Cultivated/Art Music Scene." This is perhaps not the place for a commentary on sacred music aesthetics, but discussions and exchanges clearly might serve a better understanding of the educational problems that continue to confront the church musician, particularly with regard to music from the pop culture.

As we observe the efforts of educators and politicians to deal meaningfully with the concept of multi-culturalism, and as responsible church leadership inspires our further efforts at musical ecumenism, it will be seen that there are many reasons to review our legacy of sacred music. And this is quite apart from the Quincentenary celebration of the discovery of the New World. Our own voyages of discovery must continue as we continue our journey into the Third Millenium.

Sacred Music in America
an overview

Samuel Adler

Though we constantly point to the separation of church and state guaranteed in our constitution, our country was founded by men and women to whom religion meant everything. Every aspect of their lives, including the music they sang or heard, was tied closely to their religious beliefs. Indeed, the first full-length book produced by a British North American publishing house was the *Bay Psalm Book*. This collection of psalm tunes formed the basis of New England's psalmody for more than a century. The model for the *Bay Psalm Book* was the *Ainsworth Psalter*, which the Pilgrims had brought over from Holland, and the *Sternhold and Hopkins Psalter*, which the Puritans had imported from England.

At first the *Bay Psalm Book* included no music, but rather instructed the worshipers that most of its verses could be sung either to Ravencroft's (*Whole Booke of Psalms*) tunes or to those of the *Sternhold and Hopkins Psalter*. By 1698, after nine editions, thirteen melodies with basses were finally added. This suggests that the *Bay Psalm Book*'s verses were rather elementary since they were composed in only three meters: Common Meter–8,6,8,6 syllables for a four–line verse); Long Meter–8,8,8,8; and Irregular Meter–6,6,8,6.

By the early eighteenth century, the Puritan clergy were angrily decrying the horrible state of psalm-singing in the Colonies. In 1721, one of the clergy complained that "the tunes are now miserably tortured, twisted, and disorderly noises." This protest led to reform. The Rev. John Tufts's textbook, *An Introduction to the Singing of Psalm-Tunes* (1720), appeared and explained the rudiments of music. The book also included a method of letter rather than note notation to make it easier for the average parishioner to read music. At the same time, several other texts were issued espousing the same goal. Furthermore, singing schools were established in New England (1722) as well as in New York (1754), Pennsylvania (1750), South Carolina (1730), and Maryland (1765). All these efforts resulted in a flurry of musical activity in the colonies, and native-born composers flourished. In Philadelphia in 1761, James Lyon (1735–1794) published a collection of psalm-tunes, anthems, and hymns called *Urania*. Most of the tunes were not his own but were adopted from various English psalters in circulation in the Colonies. It was here that the first "fuging" tunes appeared; these were to form the basis of the compositions by composers of the First New England School.

The First New England School was led by William Billings (1746–1800), who made his publishing debut in 1770 with *The New England Psalm-Singer* or *American Chorister*. It is interesting to note that this volume was engraved by Paul Revere. For this collection, Billings composed 108 psalms and hymns, and fifteen anthems and canons. The novelty of this publication was that he composed all of them himself instead of adapting existing tunes. From this collection, we have at least four anthems that we perform today: "When Jesus Wept," "The Rose of Sharon," "Thus Saith the High and Lofty One," and "Chester." For curiosity's sake one should look at a song called "Jargon," which Billings wrote (both words and music) in response to a criticism that he was a reactionary composer of fuging tunes. The music sounds like Stravinsky, and the words are sarcastic and angry. Billings published several other important collections (*The Singing Masters Assistant,* 1778; *The Suffolk Harmony,* 1786; and *The Continental Harmony,* 1794), from which volumes many selections have been reprinted in modern editions.

It is interesting to note that the works of Billings, Daniel Read, Samuel Holyoke, Timothy Swan, Supply Belcher, and so many others bear no resemblance to their European counterparts. After all, this was the time of Bach, Handel, Haydn, Mozart, and Beethoven, yet these had no visible influence on these "Yankee Tunesmiths" whatsoever. As Billings wrote, "I don't think myself confined to any rules for composition laid down by any that went before." These composers' melodies and harmonies were simple, flowing and folk-like in quality, and had an angular and rhythmically powerful feeling.

Before leaving the eighteenth century, we must note two other groups of church musicians who were active during this early Colonial period, but who kept themselves quite separated from the mainstream New England composers because of their own religious preference. The first group, the Pennsylvania Germans, had settled in Germantown, Pennsylvania, in 1694. Led by a clergyman named Johannes Kelpius, in their services they sang hymns, psalms, and anthems that were harmonized and arranged in a much richer and more advanced musical idiom than the examples found in either the *Bay Psalm Book* or even the works of Billings and his colleagues. There are two important early publications from this group: a hymnal that was compiled by Kelpius himself, entitled *The Lamenting Voice of the Hidden Love at the time when she lay in Misery and Forsaken,* and Johann Beissel's *The Song of the Lonely and Forsaken Turtle Dove, namely the Christian Church.* The latter, a collection of Beissel's original compositions, shows a style almost completely devoid of any dissonance on accented text syllables. While there are some antiphonal choral effects used, this lack of accented dissonance gives the music a rather bland flavor.

The other group of church musicians are the Moravians, who are still active today in providing sacred choral music. They came from German-speaking Bohemia and settled in North Carolina and Pennsylvania. Their musical life has always been intense though mostly church-centered. In the major Moravian centers such as Salem, North Carolina, and Bethlehem, Pennsylvania, there existed brass ensembles to perform at community functions. The Moravians organized *Collegia Musica* which met on a regular basis to practice both vocal and instrumental music for presentation at churches. The Moravians were also the first to establish music libraries, which they had brought over from Europe. These items included anthems, arias, motets, and chorales to be performed with and without instrumental accompaniment.

Of all the Moravian composers of that period, the finest is possibly Johann Friedrich Peter (1746–1813). Peter was the creator of almost a hundred works including many anthems and arias plus six string quintets. Peter and his colleagues John Antes (1741–1811) and David Moritz Michael (1751–1825), the most active Moravians, saw to it that the standard of music and the quality of performance was as high as possible. Michael has the great distinction of having conducted the first performance of Haydn's *The Creation* in America in 1811, only two years after the composer's death.

Though there was a noticeable increase in the number of native-born composers in the early years of the nineteenth century, there was also a greater influx of Europeans to the Colonies. This led to a proliferation of performances and publications of sacred music by the leading composers of the day, such as Handel, Haydn, Mozart, and even Beethoven. In 1815,

Gottlieb Graupner organized the Boston *Handel and Haydn Society* for the purpose of "cultivating and improving a correct taste in the performance of sacred music, and also to introduce into more general practice the works of Handel, Haydn, and other eminent composers."

The advent of the nineteenth century, with its increase in travel to and from Europe, saw the beginning of the development of secular music in the United States and an increasing number of visits by outstanding vocal as well as instrumental artists from the Old World. Choral music developed in the United States after the founding of Boston's *Handel and Haydn Society* in many of the large Eastern cities, but now the choral repertoire leaned heavily towards the Classical and early Romantic European masters.

Hymns and anthems were still composed and collected here by American-born composers. The most prolific of these collector-composers was Thomas Hastings (1784–1872), whose first collection, *Musica Sacra: A Collection of Psalm Tunes, Hymns and Set Pieces* (1815), included works of Purcell, Giardini (*Come Thou Almighty King*), William Croft, Handel, and, of course, Hastings' own original works. In this early collection, Hastings showed his proclivity for English music, but by the middle of the century he became enamored with German music and titled his 1849 hymnal *The Mendelssohn Collection*.

Certainly one of the most lasting contributions to American church music in the nineteenth century was made by Lowell Mason (1792–1872). His *Boston Handel and Haydn Society Collection of Church Music* was a tremendous success, with twenty-two editions published between 1815 and 1858. Mason also became the first American music educator, and through his influence the Boston Academy of Music was established in 1838. However, his main interest remained sacred music, and he is credited with producing over 1200 hymns and adapting almost 500 melodies by other composers (including Beethoven) for hymns to be sung in American churches.

By the end of the nineteenth century, four men and a woman had emerged as America's most outstanding composers of that period. John Knowles Paine (1839–1906), George Chadwick (1854–1931), Horatio Parker (1863–1919), Edward MacDowell (1861–1908) and Amy (Mrs. H.H.A.) Beach (1867–1944) were all born in America and finished their musical studies in Germany. They were composers of concert music, but two of them (Paine and Parker) also wrote significant sacred works.

John Knowles Paine wrote a magnificent *Mass in D* that was premiered successfully in Berlin in 1867, as well as a large oratorio, *St. Peter,* which includes accompanied chorales in the Mendelssohnian tradition. Both of these works deserve many more performances than they have received.

Horatio Parker's *Hora Novissima* (1892), a large and weighty oratorio, fared better than Paine's mass setting and remained in the repertoire until right after World War II. Parker also composed several *a cappella* Latin motets using texts by Thomas à Kempis, that are worthy of consideration.

Chadwick wrote only one large sacred work, which is entitled *Judith*. It is a sumptuous, operatic-style oratorio influenced by *Samson and Delilah* of Saint-Saëns, as well as the Wagner operatic tradition.

In 1892, Amy Beach composed a *Mass in Eb* and later on, a cantata called *Christ in the Universe*. Both of these works have long been out of print, but with renewed interest in Beach's work, they should be examined again.

Although he was the most popular of American composers of the late nineteenth century, Edward MacDowell never wrote any sacred music.

During the latter part of the nineteenth century a new development occurred in American music: the rise of the specialist. While many composers wrote both secular as well as sacred music, some were much better known for one genre than another. It is important to mention some of these American composers who contributed sacred works and whose pieces deserve much wider circulation than they are receiving today. Dudley Buck (1839–1909), Arthur Foote (1853–1937), Daniel Gregory Mason (1873–1953) and Arthur Shepherd (1880–1958) should be included in this group of sacred music composers.

At the very end of the nineteenth century, one composer stands out for his unique contribution to sacred music: Charles Ives (1874–1954). Ives based much of his compositional output on quotations from hymns and other spiritual American songs. In addition, Ives wrote some of the most beautifully effective and original psalm settings. Among these are the extraordinarily original bi-tonal setting of the 67th Psalm, as well as the tremendous setting of Psalm 90 for chorus, organ, and bells, with a low pedal C held by the organ throughout much of the work. Indeed, Ives was reported as saying that of all his works, Psalm 90 was his favorite. His setting of Psalm 24 uses mirror counterpoint and interval expansion. Of note also is a processional called *Let There Be Light*. Finally, quite a few pieces from his *114 Songs* could be used for worship services, since they have transcendentalist texts suitable for such occasions.

Before leaving the nineteenth century, one must finally mention a most important development in American church music: the increasing musical influence of the African-American church after the Civil War. Americans have profited greatly by the adoption and arrangement of spirituals and the tremendous gospel-singing movement. Early in the twentieth century, excellent arrangements of spirituals were created by such African-American composers as Frederick Work, Nathaniel Dett, William Dawson, and Harry T. Burleigh, as well as William Grant Still. Still later, Alice Parker and Robert Shaw were inspired to arrange many of these beautiful tunes. Gospel music has more recently overtaken the old spirituals in popularity and now is often the sacred music of choice in many churches in the United States.

The twentieth century has rightly been called the American century in terms of its musical development. This is certainly true in the field of sacred music. Not only is the United States the greatest consumer and customer of church music, both choral and instrumental, but also it has produced a volume of music for the church that can easily rival the output of the Baroque era. In the twentieth century, we find two types of composers: those who made their reputation in the concert hall, and those who were known only in church music circles or possibly among choral conductors. This latter group was fractured and so specialized that some composers wrote only for the Catholic Church or for the synagogue, while others wrote for specific Protestant denominations. There is a tremendous danger for anyone writing a general overview of sacred music in America since it is difficult at best to be all-inclusive. For that reason, the discussion of the twentieth century will be limited by naming the well-known masters of that era who contributed either large or small choral works to the sacred music repertoire, and then naming some trends in music written for more parochial purposes.

Of our first great American group, we find the following contributions—Aaron Copland: four early motets and *In the Beginning;* Roger Sessions: *Three Choruses on Biblical Texts* for chorus and orchestra and *Mass for Unison Choir* and

15

organ; Walter Piston: *Psalm and Prayer of David* for chorus and seven instruments; Roy Harris: *A Mass* for men's voices and organ, and many shorter sacred settings; and Randall Thompson: *The Peaceable Kingdom* (from which one can take several choruses as anthems), *Alleluia, The Last Words of David, Mass of the Holy Spirit* (*a cappella* choir), *Requiem, The Passion According to St. Luke* (huge forces including children's chorus), and many shorter sacred works.

This first group also includes Virgil Thomson: *Hymns from the Old South* ("My Shepherd" is the most famous of these) and many short sacred pieces; Howard Hanson: *The Cherubic Hymn, How Excellent is Thy Name,* settings of Psalm 150 and 121, and many more shorter sacred works; Ross Lee Finney: *Pilgrim Psalms;* Samuel Barber: *Prayers of Kierkegaard* (soprano, chorus, orchestra), *Agnus Dei* (an arrangement of the famous *Adagio for Strings*); Peter Mennin: *The Christmas Story* (an excellent work on the *Messiah* text for chorus and orchestra) and some other shorter works for chorus; Norman Dello Joio: *A Psalm of David* for chorus and orchestra, and many other sacred anthems; David Diamond: *The Young Joseph* for women's chorus and strings, *A Sacred Service* (Jewish), and many shorter anthems; and Bernard Rogers: *The Passion, The Raising of Lazarus,* and several psalm settings.

Also included in this group are Ned Rorem: *5 Prayers for the Young* for chorus, *Two Psalms and a Proverb,* and many shorter sacred choral pieces; Daniel Pinkham, one of the most prolific composers for choral and organ music for the church: *Christmas Cantata, Easter Cantata, Requiem, Stabat Mater, St. Mark Passion,* and many other shorter as well as larger sacred works; Leonard Bernstein: *Chichester Psalms, Mass, Kaddish Symphony,* and quite a few shorter works in both English and Hebrew; Robert Starer: *Ariel,* a cantata for chorus and orchestra, *Psalms of Woe and Joy,* and many shorter anthems (especially psalm settings in both Hebrew and English); Lucas

Foss: *The Song of Songs* for soprano and orchestra, and *Psalms* for two pianos or orchestra and chorus; Samuel Adler: three cantatas—*The Vision of Isaiah, The Binding, Choose Life*—and many shorter choral works in English and in Hebrew.

This is certainly not a complete list of excellent American composers who have written for the church. One must also mention such masters as Wallingford Riegger, Normand Lockwood, Vincent Persichetti, Gordon Binkerd, Ron Nelson, Dominick Argento, Marga Richter, Leo Kraft, Paul Fetler, Knut Nystedt, and Gerald Near, who have contributed so much music for the worship service. These composers, among many others, should be much better known in the general sacred music field, for their compositions could enrich and ennoble any worship service regardless of denomination.

It is also important to mention some distinguished American composers who made their reputation primarily by the creation of sacred works both large and small. Some of the earliest twentieth-century masters were Leo Sowerby, Everett Titcomb, Philip James, Katherine Davis, and (one of the most influential) Jean Berger, who has many excellent settings of biblical passages and psalms. It is certainly not the case (especially for Leo Sowerby) that these composers wrote only music for the church, but their reputations do rest mostly on the fact that their music is most often performed by choruses and organists.

There are three European composers who have had a profound influence on American sacred music of the last fifty years. The first of these was Hugo Distler, whose wonderfully evocative music, inspired by both medieval and renaissance sources, was widely performed during the middle of the twentieth century.

Heinz Werner Zimmermann made quite a splash in America with his *Psalmenkonzert* and other sacred settings accompanied by organ, double bass pizzicatos and sometimes percussion. Interestingly, these works were inspired by jazz (an American invention!) and spawned a whole series of jazz masses and services in the 1960s. These were led on by a mass by the American composer Ed Summerlin. During this tumultuous period of unrest due to the Vietnam War as well as the musical changes stemming from the pronouncements of Vatican II, there was a great flirting with aleatoric ideas that found their way into American sacred music.

Immediately thereafter, the American sacred music establishment began a rather lengthy love affair with a more calming influence: the music of the immensely popular British composer and arranger, John Rutter. His influence was quite pervasive in the latter part of the twentieth century; his works are performed more often perhaps than those of any other composer, and his influence upon American composers of sacred music is perhaps too great.

The field of sacred music in America at the beginning of the twenty-first century is a bit fractured. The movement away from classical sacred music which entered during the 1960s and 1970s has almost entirely taken over many church music programs. Choirs and organs have been replaced by congregational songs or pop-type solo singers and guitar. Of course this is by no means happening everywhere, but it is occurring with increasing frequency even in the most unlikely churches and synagogues of all communions. It is certainly not the prerogative of this author to either condone or condemn this movement. However, it is important to note that while this popular type of music seems to pervade many church music programs, important younger composers are creating inspired settings of sacred texts. To name only a few of the leading ones who have set sacred texts: Aaron J. Kernis, Michael Torke, Stephen Paulus, Morton Lauridsen, Libby Larsen, Robert Beaser, Martin Bresnick, Deborah Dratell, and Judith Zaimont, among many others.

Today, in the early years of the twenty-first century, we can only speculate as to the future of sacred music in America. This author feels that we have failed to educate our audiences when it comes to "classical" music (whether secular or sacred), and there seems to be only a slight groundswell in some quarters to counteract the intrusion of the "unadulterated popular vernacular" into our worship services. It is true that there is now some reaction to the rather mindless music that has taken over in so many houses of worship. It is unfortunate, in this author's opinion, that this music aids, abets, and parallels the improvised and often weak liturgy to which many worshipers are exposed. In a wonderful book on church music published in 1952, in a chapter entitled "The Present State," Archibald T. Davison quotes from a book entitled *The Basis of Criticism in the Arts*, by Stephen C. Pepper:

> If now it is asked, "How on any basis can a Titian be superior to a Varga (or Playboy bunny) girl?" the answer would be something like this: in the first place, any man who cannot appreciate a Varga girl is missing something. But, in the second place, a man who has not developed the discrimination to appreciate a Titian is missing something. The second man, moreover, assuming that he also appreciates a Varga, perceives that the Varga girl is little more than a paper substitute for a real girl who is much more worth appreciating than the picture of her; whereas there is no substitution for the Titian. There really is more immediate pleasure in a Titian for any man of visually refined discrimination.

While we cannot know for sure what the "visual discrimination" powers are for the average worshiper, it is disheartening to note the lack of aural discrimination in most members of congregations. Nevertheless, this author is of the firm opinion that the great words of our Judeo-Christian heritage need and deserve only the finest and most refined musical treatment, and if serious congregants are continually exposed to only the very best in sacred music, their taste can be educated to demand only that which will satisfy the spiritual self to the highest degree. Those of us concerned with the survival of great sacred music must not be discouraged by the challenge of the popular culture, but we must know that we have the repertoire to satisfy the need for an experience of profound beauty in the works of the great composers of the past and present.

Bibliography

Berger, Melvin. *Guide to Choral Masterpieces*. New York: Doubleday, 1993.

Davison, Archibald T. *Church Music*. Cambridge: Harvard University Press, 1952.

Hitchcock, H. Wiley. *Music in the United States: A Historical Introduction*. Englewood Cliffs, NJ: Prentice-Hall, 1969.

Jacobs, Arthur. *Choral Music*. Baltimore: Penguin Books, 1963.

Lowens, Irving. *Music and Musicians in Early America*. New York: W.W. Norton, 1964.

Ulrich, Homer. *A Survey of Choral Music*. New York: Harcourt Brace, 1973.

Wienandt, Elwyn A. *Choral Music of the Church*. New York: The Free Press, 1965.

The American Chorister

Craig Timberlake

The American Chorister is our designation for that choir singer who knows a considerable repertoire of sacred music by American composers and regularly enriches that knowledge through study and performance. Over the years, we at *Gloriæ Dei Cantores*, singers and staff alike, have discovered that concentration on one historical musical period or the work of a single, definitive composer helps enormously in bringing cohesion to the various elements essential to a choir's survival and growth as an indispensible component of worship. Such elements include, of course, considerations of performance practice, style, technique, and musicianship, as well as rehearsal and individual effort apart from the whole.

Recent recordings of American sacred music (as seen in the discography at the conclusion of this book) help to make our point that music of great simplicity and easy access can be maintained along with more complex works. Like a symphony's standard repertoire, the music that *Gloriæ Dei Cantores* has studied and recorded might be seen as a choir's permanent library, ranging in diversity from a unison folk hymn to a twelve-tone work such as Arnold Schoenberg's *De Profundis*, from a unison hymn by Charles Ives (see the collection *114*

Songs) to his bi-tonal setting of Psalm 67 and to his exquisite treatment of Psalm 90. Once choir members have learned to sing the whole-tone scale, the intricacies of those whole-tone clusters in Psalm 90 become relatively uncomplicated. The beauty of the unison ending hardly needs comment.

The interested reader will find in the recordings listed in the discography an American repertoire that will not only sustain interest but also promote the requisite musical growth. For individual choir members, appropriate exercises in voice production and expression can be derived from such a repertoire or from other preferred examples of similar quality. While it is clear that our efforts have been drawn from music in the classical tradition, it will also be clear to those who follow our example that we have barely exposed the riches available to a choir, whose musical life is not episodic but ongoing in the pursuit of musical and spiritual growth.

INTERNATIONAL PHONETIC ALPHABET (IPA)

In their book, *Voice Building for Choirs* (Hinshaw, 1981), Wilhelm Ehmann and Frauke Haasemann utilize the symbols of the IPA to insure correct pronunciation, enunciation, and articulation in the practice of their exercises. The use of the IPA is now so pervasive in vocal pedagogy (see Miller, 1986 and 1993; McKinney, 1994, and Odom, 1981) that to keep up with significant contributions to the literature church musicians and other voice professionals should learn to read and transcribe phonetically. Good bilingual paperback dictionaries often carry IPA transcriptions in both languages, making them useful aids to the singer who has acquired a working knowledge of the IPA symbols. Choral directors and singers will also want to acquire Kenyon and Knott's *A Pronouncing Dictionary of American English,* which provides a phonetic transcription of standard American English. In the selected readings that follow this essay, one can note more recent works by Joan Wall and others that point to a choral diction of simplicity and character, devoid of mannerism, such as is heard in *Gloriæ Dei Cantores'* recording of Aaron Copland's masterpiece, *In the Beginning.*

VOICE TEACHING IN THE CHORAL CONTEXT

Choral directors have long understood that voice teaching is an essential aspect of the rehearsal. If, as we have suggested above, the choir regularly pursues a repertoire of sacred song from simple to complex, it becomes possible for the director to continuously reinforce matters of technique in such rudiments as posture, breathing, tone quality, diction, and vowel modification. As the repertoire demands, more sophisticated understandings in regard to historical styles, accentuation, phrasing, and expression can be introduced and reinforced over time. Such an integrated choral program demands a great deal of the director, who will, in turn, recognize the available talent and expertise that can be directed toward the unending goals of musical literacy and technical development.

PEDAGOGICAL RESOURCES

For a number of years, I wrote a regular column entitled *Practica Musicae* for the *Journal of Singing,* the official organ of the National Association of Teachers of Singing. The singers of *Gloriæ Dei Cantores* were often in my mind when I addressed topics in pedagogy or performance practice. Several of these brief essays are listed in the selected readings given below. Often they attempt to reconcile pedagogical perspectives of the past and present for both teacher and singer. Other columnists in the *Journal* are among today's leading investigators and commentators on historical and current scientific literature as it pertains to singing. Choir directors interested in expanding their knowledge of current writings on singing are encouraged to subscribe to the *Journal* or borrow it from a NATS member or a public or institutional library.

Most volumes on singing (and there is a substantial increase in the number of useful texts now in print) consider major topics under these four rubrics: Respiration, Phonation, Resonation, and Articulation. James C. McKinney's new edition of his "manual for teachers of singing and choir directors," *The Diagnosis and Correction of Vocal Faults,* is indispensable. Two volumes by Richard Miller, *The Structure of Singing* (1986) and *Training Tenor Voices* (1993), are also essential reading for the choir director. Taken together, these three volumes will help the church musician not trained as a vocalist to approach such seemingly arcane topics as breath management, registers, articulation, and vowel modification.

The author has found that selected assigned readings for the choir to enhance their knowledge of physiology and anatomy relative to the human voice are of great help. Pairing choir members as teacher and student and serving as critics of interpretation and performance in repertoire classes is also of benefit. Choral directors who have not done so might consider the possibilities of peer-mediated instruction. The chamber concept is a useful place to begin. For instance, singing Billings, one voice on a part, can be highly instructive.

APPOGGIO

Traditional Italian Singing Technique

Appoggio is defined as "a technique, associated with the historic Italian school, for establishing dynamic balance between the inspiratory, phonatory, and resonatory systems in singing." See Miller (1993), *Training Tenor Voices* (p.155).

Una nobile attitudine, the singer's noble posture (axial alignment) is described by V. Manfredini in his *Regole Armoniche,* 1797. See Duey, *Bel Canto* (1951).

<u>Breath Management.</u> In *Appoggio* (*Appoggiare*-support), one differentiates the function of hypogastrium (lower abdomen) and epigastrium (upper abdomen). The diaphragm (inspiratory muscle) draws air into the lungs; it lowers some-

what to create the umbilical-epigastrial expansion at the midline. The singer maintains this expansion, thus creating the balance of power between inspiratory and expiratory muscles (lower abdominals) known in the Lamperti school as *la lotta vocale (lutte vocale)*. This delicate balance greatly assists the singer in coordinating the breath to perform a variety of tasks (range, pitch, dynamics, *messa di voce*, etc.). Breathing for singing is well described by Mengozzi, who arrived in Paris in 1787 and became professor of voice at the Paris Conservatory. See Timberlake (1994), "Apropos of Appoggio."

The term *Appoggio* constitutes a total system, encompassing sterno-costal-diaphragmatic-epigastric breathing. There is no hypogastric or lower distention here. Quiet breathing, muscular balance, ease of bearing, and avoidance of pressure anywhere are characteristic of the technique.

Sing in the position of breathing—breathe in the position of singing. Posture is not altered in the course of renewing breath. The lungs must not be crowded, and breathing is inaudible. The use of short onset exercises, while silently replenishing breath after each vowel or hum, is seen as key to elongating the breath cycle and maintaining the singer's equilibrium. Adages of *Appoggio* reinforce the importance of vital and inaudible exchanges: "The new breath is the release of the phonation." "The release is the new breath." "Sing on the gesture of inhalation." "Remain *ben appoggiata*."

Reporting on "Breathing Behavior During Singing," Johann Sundberg noted that some singers activate the diaphragm only during inhalation and for reducing subglottal pressure at high lung volumes, while other singers have been found to co-contract it throughout the breath phrase (*The NATS Journal,* Jan/Feb 1993). Sundberg told me that he preferred a co-contracting to a flaccid diaphragm. That is my preference as well. I believe that the co-contraction of the diaphragm, undertaken steadily but not aggressively, may be reasonably considered an aspect of the traditional Italian technique of *Appoggio*. Practiced diligently, it might well produce better balanced singing and breathing in fulfillment of the musical demands of the vast and diversified American repertoire from Billings to Argento.

In conclusion, it is appropriate to note the greatly expanded research available to those who deal with the professional voice in all its ramifications. While church singers may not be interested in the more arcane research of the voice scientist, there is nevertheless much to challenge their modest interest. A useful example of this would be in the realm of voice hygiene. Various scientific disciplines have in recent years revealed a remarkable fascination with the human voice. As singers, we have all learned to identify conditions that impair our good or better vocal performance. Some topics occur frequently: abuse of alcohol or tobacco; asthma, allergy, or other conditions that adversely affect the respiratorial tract. Environmental conditions now figure prominently in the assessment of our life experience as singers.

Choral methods have evolved over many years to provide a formal course of instruction in many music education programs. Behavioral studies have taught us a good deal about how people learn music. And of course our greatly increased knowledge of the physiology and anatomy of the voice has helped those of us who want to improve, enhance, and, at the same time, simplify our teaching of music for worship. Today, we see the increased use of electronic media along with more conventional methods all helping to point the way to a joyful fulfillment of our common goals as directors and choristers.

Selected Readings

VOICE

Duey, Philip A. *Bel Canto in its Golden Age: A Study of its Teaching Concepts.* New York: King's Crown Press, 1951, reprint Da Capo Press, 1980.

Gregg, Jean Westerman. "What Humming Can Do For You." *Journal of Singing,* Vol. 53, No.5, 1996.

McKinney, James. *The Diagnosis and Correction of Vocal Faults, A manual for teachers of singing and for choir directors.* Nashville: Genevox Music Group, 1994.

Miller, Richard. *The Structure of Singing.* New York: Schirmer Books, 1986.

_____. *Training Tenor Voices.* New York: Schirmer Books, 1993.

Sundberg, Johann.*The Science of the Singing Voice.*DeKalb, Illinois: Northern Illinois University Press, 1987.

_____. "Breathing Behavior During Singing." *The NATS Journal.* Vol. 50, No. 3, 1993.

Timberlake, Craig. "Pedagogical Perspectives, Past and Present. Laryngeal Positioning." *The NATS Journal.* Vol. 51, No. 1, 1994.

_____. "Pedagogical Perspectives, Past and Present: Apropos of Appoggio." *The NATS Journal.* Vol. 51, No. 2, 1994.

_____. "Pedagogical Perspectives, Past and Present: Apropos of Appoggio, II." *The NATS Journal.* Vol. 51, No. 3, 1994.

INTERNATIONAL PHONETIC ALPHABET

Cartier and Todaro. *The Phonetic Alphabet.* Dubuque, IA: Wm. C. Brown, 1983.

Kenyon, John and Thomas Knott. *A Pronouncing Dictionary of American English.* Springfield, MA: Merriam-Webster, 1953.

Marshall, Madeleine. *The Singer's Manual of English Diction.* New York: G. Schirmer, 1953.

Wall, Joan. *International Phonetic Alphabet for Singers*. Dallas: Pst...Inc., 1989.

Wall, et.al. *Diction for Singers: A concise reference for English, Italian, Latin, German, French and Spanish Pronunciation*. Dallas: Pst...Inc., 1990.

MISCELLANEOUS

Munro, Marth and Maren Larson. "The Influence of Body Integration on Voice Production." *Journal of Singing*. Vol. 52, No. 2, 1996.

Neumann, Frederick. "Authenticity and Vocal Vibrato." *New Essays in Performance Practice*. Ann Arbor, MI: UMI Research, 1989.

Sataloff, Robert T. and Ingo Titze. *Vocal Health and Science*. Jacksonville, FL: National Association of Teachers of Singing, 1991.

Titze, Ingo. "Lip and Tongue Trills—What do they do for us?" *Journal of Singing*. Vol. 53, No. 3, 1996.

_____. "More on Messa di Voce." *Journal of Singing*. March/April, 1996.

Vowels

IPA Symbol	English
[i]	we, sea
[ɪ]	give, sieve
[e]	chaos, weight
[ɛ]	when, said
[æ]	at, band, apple
[a]	valor, talon
[ɑ]	father, God, psalm
[ɔ]	awe, call, sought
[o]	robe, grove, cope
[ʊ]	book, should
[u]	soon, tune, through
[ʌ]	up, love, son, cuff, nation
[ə] (schwa)	above, parade
[ø]	learn, tern

Semi-Vowels (Glides) and Diphthongs

IPA Symbol	English
[j]	young, meow, yes, you
[w]	wish
[aɪ]	Christ, prize

IPA Symbol	English
[aʊ]	house, cowl
[ei]	way, weigh
[ɔɪ]	boy, rejoice

Consonant Sounds

IPA Symbol	Voiceless	Articulation	IPA	Voiced
[p]	Paul	bilabial	[b]	Bob
[t]	tone	lingua-alveolar	[d]	drone
[k]	cane	velar	[g]	gain
[f]	fat	labiodental	[v]	vat
[θ]	things	linguadental	[ð]	these
[s]	decease	dental	[z]	disease
[ʃ]	sh! mission	lingua-alveolar	[ʒ]	vision
[ç]	ich (German)	palatal		
[x]	ach (German)	velar		
[h]	ha - ha! (aspirate)	glottal	[ʔ] (stroke of glottis)	uh-oh!
[tʃ]	church	lingua-alveolar	[dʒ]	George
[ts]	cats	lingua-dental	[dz]	cads

Nasal Consonants

[m]	mama	bilabial nasal
[n]	nanny	lingua-alveolar nasal
[ŋ]	song	velar nasal
[ɲ]	onion (Eng)	gnocchi, lasagna (It)

Other Voiced Consonants

[ʎ]	foglia, moglie (Italian)
[l]	lull, lily, Liebe, fleur de lis, etc.
[ɹ]	rare (retroflex r)
[ř]	rolled r

Performing the Music of Our Time

James E. Jordan, Jr.

The present essay has evolved as a possible answer to the challenge of giving choirs a pathway into twentieth-century sacred music. This same challenge has required engagement with the subjective and objective sides of the church musician's art. However, it has also presented a wonderful prerequisite: the willingness to understand that the sacred classical music of our time is exactly that—*ours*.

In centuries past (and indeed, the twentieth century now qualifies for that category), the "man on the street" and "the man in the pew" were often, musically speaking, the same person. Likewise, the composers of what is referred to in this article as "classical" sacred music were composers of both the sacred and secular. Often, there simply was no division between the two categories. However, in today's culture, there is a chasm between "popular musical culture" (that which is experienced every day by the general population), and today's sacred music. Many people have not had the chance to hear, experience, or understand classical sacred music of the twentieth century as a living and meaningful vehicle for worship. Too often, the public's experience with this music is in the concert hall, and there, often, as a museum piece. It is always slightly out of reach—instead of being learned, understood, and performed on a personal level. Further, much of the standard choral repertoire comes from the "Common Harmonic Practice Period" (be it hymns, anthems, mass settings, responses, etc.), and it is this music that most choir members know and love. The words and the music have made an impression that they have combined with their own individual experiences to give meaning to a given composition. The task at hand is to offer this same possibility to the choir for learning, understanding, and performing music of our time.

As composers of the twentieth and now the twenty-first century have moved to find their individual "voices" in response to a text, a picture, a phrase, or an inspiration, they have expanded upon the uses of the basic elements of music: melody, harmony, rhythm, and form. As a result, these basic elements, possibly as simple as a scale, are used in new ways and take on sounds new to many choir members' ears. One practical way to introduce music of our century to a choir at the beginning stages of exploration is to take these same elements and study them from the standpoint of repetition and variation, demonstrating how these elements illuminate the text.

An excellent work for this type of study is Daniel Pinkham's Psalm-Motet IV: *Open To Me The Gates Of Righteousness*, which is based upon Psalm 118, verse 19, and is approximately one minute in duration. The simple and quick process of writing out the text just as the composer has set it begins to reveal the form of this piece and the words on which the composer is placing emphasis:

> Open to me the gates of righteousness
>
> of righteousness,
> the gates,
> the gates of righteousness.

I will go into them
I will go into them

and I will praise the Lord,
will praise the Lord,
will praise, will praise the Lord.

(The original from the *Revised Standard Version* of the
Holy Bible: Open to me the gates of righteousness, that I
may enter through them and give thanks to the LORD.)

Bearing in mind the responsorial structure of Hebrew poetry
(between halves of verses), one can see that the work divides
into two main sections between the words "righteousness" and
"I."

The second step is to compare the music with the text. One
quickly finds that the music in m.5, bt.4–m.11 is repeated in
mm. 16–23. This process opens three important concepts for
the choir: The music enhances what the composer has already
begun in choosing the repetition of the text, the two halves of
the work are related, and once the first section is learned, so
now is most of the second section.

MM. 1–5, bt.4	Open to me the gates of righteousness
M.5, bt.4–m.11	*of righteousness* *the gates* *the gates of righteousness.*
MM. 12–15	I will go into them I will go into them
MM. 16–23	*and I will praise the Lord,* *will praise the Lord,* *will praise, praise the Lord.*

(*italics* indicate the same music)

Following this, it is possible to do a short study of mm. 1–5 and mm. 12–15, noting especially the similarities of melodic direction and interval content between mm. 12–13 and mm. 14–15:

The following exercises are drawn from the music of these same measures. Because the scales and intervals used are those used in some form through the entire work, they can be sung on any convenient vowel and pitch. Along with the analysis, they serve to introduce the "sounds" of the work:

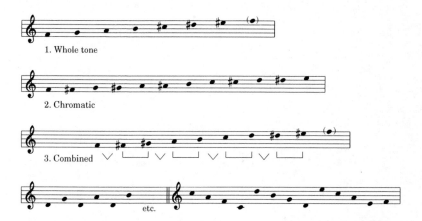

1. Whole tone

2. Chromatic

3. Combined

etc.

Upon concluding the warm-up, it is important to underscore the specific points of the subtext upon which Pinkham is expanding:

> 1) The action of praise is a result of and response to God's action of opening the gates of righteousness to the believer, as evidenced by the repetition of the text and the music.

> 2) The action of "going into them (the gates)" is a turning point for the believer, as the gates are not just opened but flung open wide, as is heard in the expanded range of the voice parts.

By giving the choir some of the composer's meaning and interpretation as seen through the analysis, the choir now has a pathway into the personal expression of the text.

Another composition that serves beautifully as an introduction to contemporary sacred music is David Ashley White's *A Lenten Prayer* for two-part chorus, organ, and treble instrument. Not unlike Pinkham's work discussed above, the overall form of this piece is accessible through the repetition of the melodic theme, which is characterized by tonal and modal qualities:

Theme: A Lenten Prayer   David Ashley White

The theme lends itself to being learned through some possible warm-up exercises made up of minor and diminished triads.

These exercises place the "sounds" of the theme into the collective "ear" of the choir. As the choir learns the main theme, their attention can be drawn to the relationship of the alternating colors of modal and tonal implications, perhaps relating the ancientness of God's love as symbolized in the modality, to modern times as represented in the tonality. This is only one possibility that will begin to give the choir a "vision" of what the composer is saying. The "B" section of the piece is a transformation of the main theme through augmentation, transposition, and major rather than minor tonal implications:

A quick aural comparison achieved by simply playing the two themes back to back with the same rhythm will allow the choir members to interpret both the textual and musical relationship of these two sections.

Thereafter, when studying the final section of the work, the choir members will have the great joy of hearing for themselves the combination of sections "A" and "B," and hearing the musical relationship underscore the textual relationship of mm. 5–13 to 38–44 and mm. 25–37 to mm. 46–49 as the person of Christ is related to "may see you face to face."

> Text: measures 25–37:
> Bring us, O Christ, to share the fullness of your joy;
> baptize us in the risen life that death cannot destroy.

Another helpful example, also by Daniel Pinkham, is Psalm-Motet IX: *Thou hast turned my laments into dancing.* This can be approached initially in a manner similar to that used in the previous works for teaching mixed meters through word accent:

> Thou hast turned my laments into dancing;
> thou hast stripped off my sackcloth and
> clothed me with joy.

Then, speaking in a quasi-waltz, 3/4 rhythm:

1 2 3 1 2 3 1 2 3 1 23
Thou hast turned my laments into dancing;

1 2 3 1 2 3 1 2 3
thou hast stripped off my sackcloth and

1 2 3 123
clothed me with joy.

At this point, a quick reminder to the choir would be in order that the key word here is "dancing," and that this dance requires a steadily pulsing eighth note—exactly what the choir was counting in the previous exercise. The exercise does two things: 1) it underscores the primacy of textual accent in this composition, and 2) it teaches the mixed meters, because Pinkham bases the changes in meter on textual accent. However, as in the previous piece, it is what the choir will have learned about the subtext that is most important: This is a dance of joy, and that is how the text should be expressed.

These are only three of the possibilities for introducing the sacred classical music of our time to our choirs. In reality, there are as many pathways into this music as there are actual pieces of music, each with its own message ready to be understood and communicated in just as familiar a manner as "the music I've sung since I was a child." With a willingness to use the basic elements of music as tools for creating a new sound for illuminating texts, choirs will move into this new century with a new love and appreciation for what has brought us thus far.

Music of the Synagogue

Samuel Adler

The music of the synagogue is at once the oldest as well as the newest of all the liturgical traditions belonging to the major religious groups of our day. It is the earliest because of the tradition recorded in the Bible in ancient times, and the most modern because of the hiatus that was imposed upon its growth and development from those early times to the Enlightenment at the end of the eighteenth century. This essay will outline parts of the earlier history of the music of the synagogue as well as provide an overview of the music of the American synagogue in greater detail.

Though the Bible is full of references to music and musical events in connection with the Temple worship, we do not know what this music sounded like, since the ancient Israelites never developed a separate musical notation. It is true that the Hebrew Bible has a system of musical accents on each word, yet it is a mystery to us regarding the actual sound of each of these accents. These accents or neumes are called *Ta'amim* and consist of circles, dashes, and other small configurations. Since the original Hebrew was written without vowels, the *Ta'amim* designate not only the word accent but often clarify its actual meaning when this is obscured by the missing vowels.

The problems today in the music for the synagogue begin with the fact that the system of musical accents, also sometimes referred to as the trope, was passed down through the ages by word of mouth. According to Eric Werner in a fascinating book entitled *The Sacred Bridge*, the music closest to the ancient Temple chant may be found in the chants of the Armenian Church. Because of its longevity and its isolation, the Armenian Church protected and codified its chants as far back as the third century. This was the historical period during which the Armenians converted from Judaism to Christianity.

From the time of the destruction of the Second Temple in Jerusalem by the Romans in AD 70, we have the growth of the synagogue as a substitute for the Temple worship as well as for the Temple sacrifices. In addition, prayer services in the synagogues were named after the sacrifices offered at precise times in the ancient Temple. The services were entitled morning prayer (*Shacharit*), afternoon prayer (*Minsha*), and evening prayers (*Maaviv*). On Sabbaths and Holy Days an extra set of prayers was offered, which, when added to the morning prayer, again recalled a sacrifice. These were called *Musaf*, and while no translation is available, this was the special Holy Day sacrifice it represented.

Since it was a Talmudic decree that all prayers had to be chanted, a presentor or *Sh'liach Tsibbur* (a representative of the congregation, later called a cantor) was chosen to chant the prayers and lead the congregation in antiphonal songs. We do not know anything about the sound of these songs or chants, though we do have verbal descriptions that they were simple and beautiful. In this time period, there was also a strict ban decreed by the rabbis on any instrumental music in the worship service. Two reasons were given for this prohibition: to mourn for the destruction of the Temple, which had had a profusion of instrumental music, and (and this one is much more important) so that the pagan rituals celebrated with instruments by Israel's neighbors would not find their way into the synagogue.

As the Jews were dispersed into Europe and Northern Africa, they took with them the institution of the synagogue, which became central in their lives. The chants that each pre-sentor (or by that time called *Chazzan*) carried in his head became a sacred tradition. Here one may ponder the use of the word "traditional." Because none of these chants were notated, and all of them passed from generation to generation by word of mouth, each country and even each small area of a country developed its own "tradition" sacred to itself. The main traditions (which have within them many variations) were the Sephardic, or southern European and North African, and the Ashkenazic, or central and eastern European tradition.

Looking back on these traditions, which had their music notated subsequently by non-Jewish scholars during the Middle Ages, one is able to detect similarities in many musical gestures and phrases. By the Middle Ages, these tunes had been tremen-dously influenced by the music of the country where these particular Jews lived in both Europe and Africa. In addition, beginning about the ninth century in Europe (except in Spain), the Jews were forced to live in segregation from the rest of the population in ghettos and were forbidden to study music of any kind. It is astounding that during all of the wonderful musical developments of the Middle Ages through the Classical period, Jews were barred from taking part in any musical activity save their own traditional chant-like music.

Indeed, there was only one exception, and that was in the sixteenth century when the Duke of Mantua (Italy) permitted a talented young Jew to study music. He was Salomone Rossi (1570–1628), a gifted composer and harpsichordist who set Hebrew psalms and prayers of the synagogue to music. These settings are either for male chorus or mixed chorus *a cappella* ranging from two-part to ten-part choirs. The rabbis of the period (except for those in Mantua) saw this kind of music as a threat to tradition. It was not until the middle of the nineteenth century that Rossi was rediscovered, and now there is a renewed interest in his music.

It was only with the dawning of the Enlightenment that Europe's Jews were enfranchised, mostly by Napoleon, and movements arose to reform both the worship as well as the music of the synagogue. One can date these developments to around the year 1800.

Throughout these dark ages, an element most important to the development and continuity of music in the synagogue was the position of the cantor. At first, he was the most highly honored man in the community. He is described by Rabbi Judah in the *Talmud* as "a man who has heavy family obligations, but who has not enough to meet them; who has to struggle for a livelihood, but who nonetheless keeps his house clean and above reproach; who has an attractive appearance, is humble, pleasant, and liked by people; who has a sweet voice, and musical ability; who is well-versed in the Scriptures, capable of preaching, conversant with *Halacha* (Law) and *Agada* (Folklore); and who knows all the prayers and benedictions by heart." This is indeed a description of a saint, and a description almost impossible to meet.

This position was quickly modified, the essential quality remaining that of a sweet voice, which was considered a divine gift capable of moving and inspiring the people to devotion. Since the lot of the Jews during these centuries was a tragic one, the cantor's prayers to God more and more echoed the lament of the people and frequently moved the congregation to tears. It is this aspect of Jewish liturgical music which, regrettably, most Jews and most non-Jews still look upon as representing a genuine tradition. In this author's estimation, this mistaken notion has dealt the harshest blow to the growth of a new synagogue music that would appropriately reflect contemporary life.

We may now turn specifically to the American synagogue, where music became an important issue only after 1850. The Spanish-Portuguese community of seventeenth-century America was relatively unimportant for two reasons: its extremely small size, and its loyalty to Sephardic traditions established in Spain during the fourteenth and fifteenth centuries.

The new immigrants from Germany arriving in America in the middle of the nineteenth century faced a totally different situation. Dominated in their thinking by the Age of Enlightenment, they embarked upon a life of freedom never envisioned before by any Jewish group, and they were impatient to bring about many changes. As Dr. D. Philipson put it, "Whatever makes us ridiculous before the world as it now is, may be and should be abolished, and whatever tends to elevate the divine service to inspire the heart of the worshiper and to attract him, should be done without unnecessary delay." Music, of course, was one of the first elements most vitally affected.

Aside from importing a few cantors (for instance, Jacob Frainkel, 1808–1887, and Alois Kaiser, 1840–1908), the newly formed American congregations, especially in the South, deleted all traces of their musical inheritance and were perfectly willing to turn over the reins of music in the American Reform synagogue to Gentile organists and music directors. These men set the prayers, with reverence and dignity, to the best available church tunes, and to some "traditional" German tunes that they found in the Sulzer collections and in the German-Jewish hymnals available in this country. The hymnal edited by Alois Kaiser, which was published by the Central Conference of American Rabbis in 1897, contained two tunes each by Sulzer and Lewandowsky, and one by Kirschner; the rest were adaptations of German, French, and English church hymns.

The only Jewish musician who was able to gain any acclaim during this period was Sigmund Schlesinger. Born and educated in Germany, he came to America in 1860 and settled in Mobile, Alabama. There he served the Reform congregation for 40 years and composed all the choir responses and prayers contained in the *Union (Reform) Prayer Book*. Regrettably, his influence lingers into our time. His compositions are of mediocre quality, borrowing heavily from the music of the Lutheran church (for melodies in the major mode) and from eighteenth-century Italian opera (for melodies in the minor mode). Musically a bit better and more attentive to Jewish tradition were his contemporaries Sparger, Stark, Grauman, and Grimm.

Four events in American Jewish life changed this less than ideal situation. The first was the great migration of Eastern European Jews to this country; they brought with them their traditional music, which through some talented musicians among their group found its way into the Reform movement of America as did, in fact, many of their number during the early part of the twentieth century. The second was the scholarship of A.Z. Idelsohn, who published his *Thesaurus of Hebrew-Oriental Melodies* in ten volumes, a veritable treasure house of tunes collected in Europe and the Middle East. The third was the excellent training of young American Jews, the sons of immigrants who, through a renewed interest in music by the American Reform and Conservative movements, were able to find positions as music directors in temples and synagogues. And finally, the fourth was the new immigration of German and other European Jews fleeing Hitler's advance and bringing with them a great knowledge of tradition as well as an excellent education in music.

These events may be summarized by saying that an interest in the musicological studies of ancient Jewish chants by Idelsohn, Werner, and Yasser, as well as a genuine flowering and pride of the American Jewish community, led to a movement devoted to the promulgation of a liturgical music for the synagogue that is meaningful, contemporary, and yet traditional.

Two general problems present themselves immediately to the composer of today's Jewish liturgical music: the choice of "traditional" melodic material, and the ever-present enigma of suitable harmony. An examination of these problems is imperative in this discussion. Through research into the trope and its usage throughout the world, and by an analysis of Jewish song both in and out of the synagogue for the past three or four hundred years, it has been concluded that the bulk of our liturgical material seems to be based on three modes which, having originated in the recitation of the synagogue prayer, were given names of prayer chants:

1. The "Adonay Malach" mode (The Lord Reigneth) derives its name from the 93rd Psalm, which is one of the opening psalms of the Friday eve liturgy. It is a modified Mixolydian scale with a major third and a minor tenth.

The two forms of the third based on the final c and of the second approaching the final c are not interchangeable. This mode is traditionally used for the psalms of praise in the Sabbath eve liturgy and in the prayers of the High Holy Days; it has a strong, "outgoing" quality.

2. The "Magen Avot" mode (Shield of the Fathers) takes its name also from a prayer found in the Sabbath eve

liturgy. It is a "pure" mode formed after the Aeolian scale.

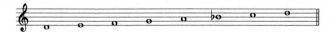

The prayers set to this mode are usually of a quiet, reflective, and peaceful mood.

3. The "Ahavah Rabbah" mode (With Great Love) is the only one to which no biblical chant derivation can be attributed. It might be considered a modified Phrygian scale.

The name is derived from a Sabbath morning liturgy prayer that has been used widely and even indiscriminately The mode has its origin in Eastern European folk music; rather than having been engendered by synagogue song, the mode was superimposed upon the synagogue song by cantors from that area. Regrettably, it is the mode most frequently used, and thus the sound of the augmented second is superficially equated with Jewish liturgical music. Its popularity is further enhanced by its frequent appearance in the popular folk songs of Eastern Europe, especially those of the Chassidim.

It must be pointed out that the concept of a mode is not the same as that of a scale. The term *mode*, to quote Isadore Freed, "is to be understood as applying to certain melismatic patterns within a fixed scale, as well as to the special devotional mood inherent in the prayers for which a given mode is used."

This, then, is the first source of tradition to which the modern composer has been able to turn, as is evidenced by excellent examples of liturgical music of American synagogue composers whose inspiration has been guided by the characteristics inherent in these modes.

L'chu N'ran'na (Psalm 95) Adonay Malach mode from "Sabbath Morning Liturgy" by Heinrich Schalit

Magen Avot (Shield of the Fathers) Magen Avot mode from "Nachlat Israel" by Hugo Ch. Adler

The choice of melodic material is not entirely limited to these modal patterns, though it may be related to them. There are three other general possibilities:

(1) Settings of prayers, especially those containing passages from the Bible, to actual biblical tropes.

Lo Yarev (They Shall Not Hurt) Prophetic Cantillation from "Kabbalath Shabbath" by A.W. Binder

(2) Arrangements and adaptations of melodies evolving from the oral traditions in the diverse countries where the Jews were scattered.

L'Cha Dodi (Beloved Come) Portuguese Tradition from "Avodat Shabbat," Friday Evening Service by Herman Berlinski

(3) Original tunes freely utilizing elements of all of the mentioned sources and offering, of course, the finest possibility for genuine achievement to a composer of liturgical music.

Tov L'hodot (Psalm 92) from "Avodat Shabbat" by Herbert Fromm

In turning to the second general problem in the composition of works for the American synagogue, that of harmony, it has to be remembered that chant by its very nature and function calls for unison singing and thus defies treatment by traditional harmonic devices that grew up during the "common practice period." Nineteenth-century Jewish composers such as Lewandowsky, Sulzer, Weintraub, and Gerovitch were overwhelmed by this seeming enigma, and simply compromised their lack of knowledge concerning modal structure by setting traditional chants to the only kind of harmony they knew: Romantic harmony. More often than not they changed the modal character of the tune by adding their kind of "musica ficta," a major dominant chord which they found was nonexistent in any of the traditional modes. If they left the chant in its original form, they fumbled aimlessly with cumbersome modulatory devices. Not so the composer of the twentieth century. Well versed in contemporary harmony as well as in the contrapuntal devices of the sixteenth century and earlier periods, he proved himself more able in handling the problem of harmony connected with modal melodies and chants.

Through a study of the music by recent synagogue composers, some interesting harmonic and contrapuntal trends emerge:[1]

(1) Sparse harmonic treatment which is, of course, a reaction against the tyranny of the continuously "fat" four-part harmony of our nineteenth-century pioneers. The treatment of melismatic as well as syllabic chants in two or three parts provides a harmonic structure that gives the melody a chance to crystallize.

Grant Us Peace from "Adath Israel" by Herbert Fromm

Tzur Yisrael (Rock of Israel) from "Sacred Service" by Ernest Bloch

---

[1] On this subject, Isadore Freed has written an excellent book entitled *Harmonizing the Modes* published by the Sacred Music Press. 1 West 4th St., New York, NY, 10012.

(2) The use of extensive unison or octave passages allowing free reign for an implied harmony by overtones, and a new type of organum and fauxbourdon which lends the modal song a much stronger interpretation.

Yism'chu from "Adath Israel" by Herbert Fromm

(3) Apparent abandonment of traditional harmonic treatment by some of our foremost composers who have substituted purely contrapuntal devices that aptly fit the character of traditional melodies.

V'shamru (Thou Shalt Keep the Sabbath) from "Shabbat Shalom" by Julius Chajes

Silent Devotion ("Song of Songs" Cantillation) from "Avodat Shabbat" by Herbert Fromm

(4) A sensitivity for modal harmony by which our composers have been able to clothe both the inspiring chant and the commonplace pseudo-oriental melody with dignified and elevating harmonic setting.

V'shamru from "Sabbath Eve Liturgy" by Heinrich Schalit

Mi Chamocha from "Avodat Shabbat" by Herbert Fromm

A new set of criteria and several groups of composers entered the field of synagogue music and Jewish music in general during the last four decades of the twentieth century. The first group of composers to be discussed has followed the example of such outstanding creators as Bloch, Milhaud, and Castelnuova-Tedesco. In other words, these composers have written excellent music for Jewish occasions, but at the same time have distinguished themselves mostly on the strength of their reputation in the secular or concert music they have produced. Such men as Hugo Weisgall, David Diamond, Arthur Berger, David Amram, Ernst Levy, Ernst Toch, Leonard Bernstein, Robert Starer, Jacob Druckman, Michael Horvit, and Yehudi Wyner, and women such as Miriam Gideon, Judith Zaimont, Sheila Silver, Janice Hamer, and many others have contributed large amounts of music directly to the repertoire of the synagogue liturgy, as well as many works based on liturgical texts. These works are of the highest musical standards, but many of them naturally do not take into consideration the practical musical limitations of the average performing groups in the synagogue today. To this group belong a long list of young Jewish composers who are firmly planted in the secular world, but like their non-Jewish counterparts often express their spiritual side by composing music for the synagogue or by setting other sacred texts.

Most Reform and Conservative Temples today have well trained cantors, but except for High Holy Day services or other special occasions they do not employ professional choirs, nor have they succeeded in encouraging amateur choirs capable of high musical achievement. There are a few exceptions to this rule in some of the larger American cities, but generally the choral situation in most of today's synagogues is not encouraging.

Because of this situation, a second group of composers has emerged. These men and women have tried to serve this large constituency with fine and usually tasteful music, setting the liturgy with both traditional Jewish tunes and chants as well as their own inventions often based on "the new romanticism," jazz and "new age" elements, and some melodic popular influences of the latter twentieth century. The leading composers in this group are Ben Steinberg, Jack Gottlieb, Charles Davidson, Jerome Kopman, William Scharlin, Bonia Shur, Stephen Richards, Simon Sargon, Aminadav Aloni, and Michael Isaacson.

This group of composers has quite a few traits in common: they are all well trained in composition and well versed in the Hebrew language; they all have been actively engaged professionally in the synagogue either as cantors, organists, or music directors; and all of them have written a large amount of Jewish liturgical music and have utilized many tunes from a variety of world Jewish communities for use in the synagogue as well as other Jewish institutions.

In order to understand this style both melodically and harmonically, here follow some short, but representative excerpts from their music. The treatment of the tunes is much less contrapuntal than that used by the synagogue composers of the earlier twentieth century, and the harmony is less distinctive in comparison to the work of Fromm, Freed, or Schalit.

Shalom Rav-B'sefer Chayim

Ben Steinberg

Sim Shalom

Michael Isaacson

R'tzei

Stephen Richards

Mi Sheshikein

Jack Gottlieb

Uv'chein Tein Kavod

Aminadav Aloni

Lo Yisa Goi

Charles Davidson

The next group of composers is made up mostly of cantors and music directors who are not primarily composers. The most notable of these are Mary Feinsinger, Benji Schiller, Don Gurney, Lauri Corrsin, David Goldstein, Laurence Avery, David Lefkowitz, Jeff Klepper and Jill Higgins. Many of these men and women are tunesmiths, and their works are harmonized and arranged by other composers or arrangers. Others such as Schiller, Feinsinger, and Higgins are trained in compositional skills and write their own original works. The sound of this music is quite traditional with slightly modal harmony, but related to a stereotypical "Jewish" sound. In many cases this means using Chassidic or modern Israeli prototypes and embracing a folk-like idiom that is easy for any congregation to understand.

V'ye-etayu-All the World

Benjie-Ellen Schiller

Shehecheyanu

Lori Corrsin

The final group of composers is one that is perhaps too pervasive in the synagogue at the beginning of the twenty-first century; these are the voices that originate in the summer camp songs. These songs are repetitive, bland, and harmonically static. These characteristics even pertain to those songs that are spirited and rhythmic. Most of this music is written by men and women who have no formal musical training and are accompanied by guitar. The most famous of these creators is Debbie Friedman, who has a gift for lyricism, but whose songs are mostly nostalgic and, like the creations of the others in this group, sound much the same.

While these camp songs are excellent for use around the "friendship circle" in the religious camps run by the Reform and Conservative movements, they have begun to supplant the music of the other groups of composers discussed in this chapter.

Here is perhaps the most popular tune to come from this group of composers. It is used extensively in all Reform congregations for the "healing" service that has been introduced throughout the country.

Mi Shebeirach   Debbie Friedman

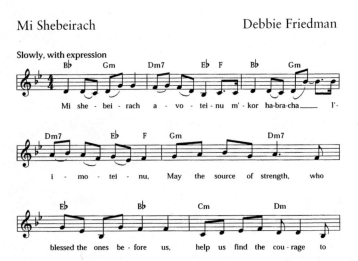

The reason for the lack of discussion of music in the synagogues around the world outside of the United States is that since the destruction of much of European Jewry during the Holocaust, synagogue music in Europe and Israel is not very creative. The reason for this situation is that almost all of the congregations in Europe and Israel are of the orthodox persuasion, and their music is based on chants developed especially during the eighteenth and nineteenth centuries in either eastern or western Europe. Since then, not much has changed, but now there are signs, especially in England, in Germany, as well as in Israel, where more liberal congregations are being formed, that a promise of a more creative approach to music may be in the future.

It is difficult to predict what will happen to the music of the synagogue in the twenty-first century, but it is safe to say that it has been greatly enriched by many outstanding twentieth-century masters who have bequeathed ennobling music of the highest quality to the synagogue. On the other hand, most of this music is not heard in today's worship service, and a turgid, monotonous pseudo-pop repertory created by mostly amateur composers has become standard fare in most temples and synagogues. This latter situation is due largely to the fact that most congregations are not able to create choruses of any quality with the ability to cope with anything more than unison or, occasionally, two to three part simple arrangements. It is hoped that this will change, and if it does, it is heartening to realize that there exists a repertory of beautiful and expert music that is readily available to be performed. The music created in the past 200 years should be the basis for a renewal of the music for the synagogue in the twenty-first century and beyond.

This article originally appeared in American Choral Review, Volume VI, Nos. 3 and 4, *April and July 1964, and has been altered and updated for this book. For more information, please contact The American Choral Foundation c/o Chorus America, 1156 15th St. N.W., Suite 310, Washington, D.C. 20005-1704; www.chorusamerica.org.*

A Selected and Annotated Bibliography

David Chalmers

This bibliography is prepared as a guide to books, articles, recordings, and Internet Web sites that would serve as basic reference materials and springboards for further thought in American sacred music. This bibliography is meant only as a starting point: Many of the resources listed here have excellent and sometimes exhaustive bibliographies.

BOOKS

Brown, Howard Mayer, ed. *Performance Practice: Music After 1600.* New York: W.W. Norton,1989.

    A splendid resource that covers a wide range of performance practice topics. Part III (chapters 16–21) covers the Romantic period. Wayne Leupold has written very thoroughly on organ performance practice, and there are interesting sections on the voice and how it was used in nineteenth and twentieth-century music.

Broyles, Michael. *"Music of the Highest Class"—Elitism and Populism in Antebellum Boston.* New Haven: Yale University Press, 1992.

    This fascinating book deals with the duality in American culture between classical music and popular music. Mr. Broyles uses a social-historical perspective to describe musical life in early nineteenth-century Boston. He traces the history of the theory that classical music is a morally positive influence and has the power to enrich people's lives.

Chase, Gilbert. *America's Music from the Pilgrims to the Present.* New York: McGraw-Hill, 1955.

This is probably the best known single volume history of American music. It is especially rich in detail about the early history of American music and is helpful in delineating the early threads that make up our sacred music heritage.

DeVenney, David P. *American Choral Music Since 1920.* Berkeley: Fallen Leaf Press, 1993.

_____. *American Masses and Requiems—A Descriptive Guide.* Berkeley: Fallen Leaf Press, 1990.

_____. *Nineteenth-Century American Choral Music: An Annotated Guide.* Berkeley: Fallen Leaf Press, 1987.

For anyone looking for specific American sacred music, these volumes are invaluable. Each volume is exhaustive in its chosen subject matter, and contains valuable details about hundreds of works. The volumes also contain annotated bibliographies of books and articles. As research helps, these three volumes are invaluable.

Ellinwood, Leonard. *The History of American Church Music.* New York: DaCapo, 1970.

This famous book covers the background of American sacred music more thoroughly than any other. It uses the *Episcopal Hymnal 1940* as a basis for showing the eclecticism of American hymnody and the melting pot of influences on American sacred music.

Ewen, David. *American Composers: A Biographical Dictionary.* New York: G.P. Putnam's Sons, 1982.

This is a beautifully written and compiled book that features hundreds of American composers. Each entry includes an extensive biography, a bibliography, a list of principal works, and, most interesting, a section called "The Composer Speaks," which gives each composer an opportunity to reflect on his methods of composition.

Gleason, Harold and Warren Becker. *Early American Music: Music in America from 1620 to 1920.* Bloomington, IN: Frangipani Press, 1981.

This volume is from an important series of music history outlines. Like its companion volumes, this book deals with the subject in great depth and provides great detail even in obscure matters. It also contains extensive bibliographies.

Hall, Charles J. A. *Chronicle of American Music 1700-1995*. New York: Schirmer Books, 1996.

In this recent book, each year is broken down into several categories: history (American and world), art and literature, and both "vernacular" and "cultured" music. This book is invaluable for the all-inclusive perspective it gives in detailing the American cultural scene over nearly 300 years.

Hitchcock, H. Wiley and Stanley Sadie, eds. *The New Grove Dictionary of American Music*. New York: MacMillan Press, 1986.

This is the multi-volume reference (four volumes) that is an offshoot of the *New Grove Dictionary of Music and Musicians*. There is no other reference like it covering so many relevant subjects; it is especially good in biographical and bibliographical detail.

Kingman, Daniel. *American Music: A Panorama*. New York: Schirmer Books, 1998.

This is a recent updating of this popular music textbook. It succeeds in showing the history of American music through different trends and genres rather than focusing on a chronological approach.

Krummel, D.W., Jean Geil, Doris J. Dyen, and Deane L. Root. *Resources of American Music History: A Directory of Source Materials from Colonial Times to World War II*. Chicago: University of Illinois Press, 1981.

Krummel, D.W. *Bibliographic Handbook of American Music*. Chicago: University of Illinois Press, 1987.

These two books are wonderful resources for finding information on just about any aspect of American music, secular and sacred. The first book is organized by state, listing libraries, universities, institutions, and private collections that contain important documents pertaining to American music. The second book is organized by chronology, context, genre (a separate section on sacred music), and bibliographic forms. These references are valuable for both the student and scholar of American music.

Lambert, Barbara. *Music in Colonial Massachusetts 1630–1820 II: Music in Homes and Churches*. Boston: The Colonial Society of Massachusetts, 1985.

This is the second of two volumes that publish the papers delivered at a conference held by the Colonial Society of Massachusetts in May, 1973. There is a wealth of information here, particularly chapters on the singing-schools and the songsters that came from them, early American psalmody, and eighteenth–century organs.

Lowens, Irving. *Music and Musicians in Early America.* New York: W.W. Norton, 1964.

Written by one of our leading scholars on American music, this series of essays on various topics and composers leads one into early America with great authenticity and style.

Orr, N. Lee and W. Dan Hardin. *Choral Music in Nineteenth-Century America: A Guide to the Sources.* Lanham, MD: The Scarecrow Press, Inc., 1999.

This is an excellent resource for many aspects of nineteenth-century sacred music in America. There are sections on Moravian music and on hymns and gospel songs and shape-notes, as well as on individual composers such as Dudley Buck, George Chadwick, and John Knowles Paine. The leaning here is scholarly, but there is much of interest for the choir director looking to expand a choir's repertoire beyond the familiar.

Potter, John, ed. *The Cambridge Companion to Singing.* Cambridge University Press, 2000.

This book is part of a large series focusing on individual composers as well as musical topics of general interest. This particular volume deals with a number of topics ranging from pop music to an excellent description of the human voice. Choir directors will find other essays on performance practices, children's singing, and teaching to be especially valuable. There is also a fine essay on American sacred music by Neely Bruce that is especially interesting for its description of spirituals and gospel music.

Stevenson, Robert. *Protestant Church Music in America.* New York: W.W. Norton, 1966.

This book is an excellent companion volume to the Ellinwood book mentioned above. It is a brief but invaluable survey, covering a broad range of history and musical developments.

Struble, John Warthen. *The History of American Classical Music.* New York: Facts on File, 1995.

This recent volume argues that there really is a truly American classical music, and that we have our own unique tradition, free from European or other influences. This volume gives details about many composers and their styles.

Tawa, Nicholas E. *The Coming of Age of American Art Music*. New York: Greenwood Press, 1991.

This is an important book, as it seeks to provide a defense for the European-influenced New England Classicists. Tawa succeeds in giving the reader a proper frame of reference for this era; the detail about such composers as Paine, Chadwick, Foote, and others is enlightening. However, he spends little time talking about their sacred music (Dudley Buck is all but forgotten), and this weakens the validity of his premise. Nevertheless, this is a book that fills in many holes of our knowledge of post-Civil War musical America.

Wienandt, Elwyn A. *Choral Music of the Church*. New York: The Free Press, 1965.

The author's purpose in this book is to bring together the principal developments of Christian choral music from many centuries. Pages 349-356, 397-409 and 429-440 are particularly relevant to American sacred music and are well worth exploring.

Articles

For the choir director exploring American choral repertoire, perhaps the most accessible and up-to-date resource is the music periodical. For many years, the periodicals of choice have been *The Choral Journal*, *The American Organist*, and *The Diapason*. Within these periodicals, interested choir directors will find columns devoted to music reviews and articles pertaining to specific composers as well as performance practices and voice pedagogy. A local public or college library can assist those looking for specific issues and articles of these and other related periodicals.

Recordings

The following list is highly selective and is not meant to be comprehensive. Rather, it is a sampling of currently available recordings of high quality in both performance and sound that will give choir directors a point of departure in selecting sacred repertoire for their own groups. A look at the most recent issue of the Schwann *Opus* catalog will yield further possibilities.

The Boston Camerata, Joel Cohen, director.

Their numerous recordings include several devoted to American sacred music of the late eighteenth and nineteenth centuries as well as a most interesting recording devoted to Shaker chants and spirituals:

The American Vocalist: Spirituals and Folk Hymns, 1850–1870.
Erato 2292-45818-2.
An American Christmas: Carols, Hymns and Spirituals,
1770–1870. Erato 2292-92874-2.
Simple Gifts: Shaker Chants and Spirituals.
Erato 4509-98491-2
Trav'ling Home: American Spirituals 1770–1870.
Erato 0630-12711-2

Gloriæ Dei Cantores, Elizabeth Patterson, director.
This choir has also recorded extensively; among their recordings are three focused on American sacred music:
Make His Praise Glorious: American Psalmody—
Volume I. Gloriæ Dei Cantores 025 Music of Samuel Adler, Charles Ives, Daniel Pinkham, Randall Thompson, Robert Starer, and others.
By the Rivers of Babylon: American Psalmody—
Volume II. Gloriæ Dei Cantores 027 Music of Virgil Thomson, Bruce Neswick, Charles Loeffler, Arnold Schoenberg, Gerald Near, Kent Newbury, and others.
Aaron Copland and Virgil Thomson: Sacred and Secular Choral Music. Gloriæ Dei Cantores 029 Music includes Copland's *In the Beginning* and Thomson's *Hymns from the Old South.*

Kansas City Chorale, Charles Bruffy, director.
This choir has recorded a varied repertoire on the Nimbus label; their discs include the following of interest:
Nativitas (music by Conrad Susa, Ned Rorem, Leo Sowerby, Norman Dello Joio, Henry Cowell, and others)
Nimbus 5413.
Alleluia: An American Hymnal. **Nimbus 5568.**

Robert Shaw Festival Singers, Robert Shaw, director.
The late Robert Shaw was well known for his many arrangements (often with Alice Parker) of American hymns and spirituals; several of these can be found on this disc:
Amazing Grace: American Hymns and Spirituals.
Telarc 80325.

Two additional discs are of interest for American repertoire:
Lost Music of Early America: Music of the Moravians.
Boston Baroque, Martin Pearlman, director. **Telarc 80482.**

"A Land of Pure Delight": *William Billings, Anthems and Fuging Tunes*. His Majestie's Clerkes, Paul Hillier, director. **Harmonia Mundi** 907048

A new label of great interest for American repertoire is **Arsis**. Their Web site can be found at *www.arsisaudio.com*. Recordings of the American Repertory Singers under the direction of Leo Nestor can be found here as well as recordings of contemporary American music.

WEB SITES

This is an exciting development of recent years, but to keep current with the numerous sites takes patience and time! For the choral director, an indispensible Web site is www.choralnet.com. Here one can find a wealth of information and links to other important Web sites (such as the one for the American Choral Directors Association, ACDA). For American music, the American Music Center has a Web site, www.amc.net, that will keep the choir director informed of the latest trends and thinking in American music.

Another useful Web site along these lines is American Music Links: home.olemiss.edu/~mudws/amlinks.html. A link to numerous music publishers is TCMR Communications Inc.: www.tcmr.com. An important series of American music reprints is now in progress through the Library of Congress Choral Series. This can be found at Walton Music's Web site: www.waltonmusic.com. Publisher's Web sites are of particular help and interest in finding online catalogs and information about specific composers. A few of the important ones are (and this is a strictly personal selection): www.presser.com (Theodore Presser), www.ecspublishing.com (E.C. Schirmer), www.boosey.com (Boosey and Hawkes), and www.etranscon.com (Transcontinental Music Publications). Almost all major publishers have their own Web sites and directors are strongly encouraged to take advantage of this information which is now so conveniently and quickly found.

One other resource must be mentioned even at the risk of overstating the obvious: our colleagues. With the use of e-mail now so prevalent, it is much easier to contact our colleagues in church music and exchange ideas and resources that will be of help and interest. In conclusion, it should be noted that the listings above should be considered as a basis for further reading and listening. It will be of great satisfaction to the author to know of other important resources that others may find, and if this listing of sources proves stimulating in this way, then it will have served its purpose.

Notes on Contributors

Samuel Adler was born in Mannheim, Germany, and came to the United States in 1939. He holds a B.M. from Boston University, an M.A. from Harvard University, and four honorary doctorates from other institutions. Dr. Adler has composed some 400 works in all media, and has published three books: *Choral Conducting* (1985), *The Study of Orchestration* (1989), and *Sight Singing* (1997). From 1966–1994 he was professor of composition at the Eastman School of Music, and he is currently on the faculty of the Juilliard School.

David Chalmers is an assistant conductor of *Gloriæ Dei Cantores* as well as an artist-in-residence. He holds degrees in organ performance from Westminster Choir College (B.M.) and the Eastman School of Music (M.M. and D.M.A.). Dr. Chalmers has also studied nineteenth–century organs and their music, thanks to a Fulbright fellowship.

James E. Jordan, Jr. is a graduate of Southern Methodist University (B.M.) and the Eastman School of Music (M.M. and D.M.A.) in organ performance. He is presently an assistant conductor of *Gloriæ Dei Cantores* and is also an artist-in-residence. He is the director of the music theory program for the *Gloriæ Dei Artes Foundation* performing groups.

Daniel Pinkham was born in Massachusetts and received his A.B. and M.A. degrees from Harvard University. He is the recipient of six honorary degrees as well as numerous awards and fellowships for his compositions. He is on the faculty of the New England Conservatory of Music and is Music Director Emeritus at historic King's Chapel in Boston. Pinkham's compositions include numerous works for choir and voice.

74

Craig Timberlake taught for many years at Teachers College, Columbia University. He is also a past president of the New York Singing Teachers Association. As a bass soloist, Dr. Timberlake appeared with the Bach Aria Group, the New York City Opera, the Handel and Haydn Society, and the Robert Shaw Chorale, among others. He has also premiered many works by American composers. Dr. Timberlake currently serves as a musical consultant to *Gloriæ Dei Cantores*.

Permissions Acknowledgments